# The Most Wanted Healthy Air Fryer Cookbook

## Do Yourself a Big Favor with this Book

*By*

Caroline Taylor

# Table of content

# Aromatic Baked Potatoes with Chives

(Ready in about 45 minutes | Servings 2)

**Per serving:**

434 Calories; 14.1g Fat; 69g Carbs; 8.2g Protein; 5.1g Sugars

## Ingredients

4 medium baking potatoes, peeled 2 tablespoons olive oil

1/4 teaspoon red pepper flakes

1/4 teaspoon smoked paprika 1 tablespoon sea salt

2 garlic cloves, minced

2 tablespoons chives, chopped

## Directions

Toss the potatoes with the olive oil, seasoning, and garlic.

Place them in the Air Fryer basket. Cook in the preheated Air Fryer at 400 degrees F for 40 minutes or until fork tender.

Garnish with fresh chopped chives. Bon appétit!

# Baked Spicy Tortilla Chips

(Ready in about 20 minutes | Servings 3)

**Per serving:**

189 Calories; 5.1g Fat; 30.7g Carbs; 4.7g Protein; 2g Sugars

## Ingredients

6 (6-inch) corn tortillas 1 teaspoon canola oil

1 teaspoon salt

1/4 teaspoon ground white pepper 1/2 teaspoon ground cumin

1/2 teaspoon ancho chili powder

## Directions

Slice the tortillas into quarters. Brush the tortilla pieces with the canola oil until well coated.

Toss with the spices and transfer to the Air Fryer basket.

Bake at 360 degrees F for 8 minutes or until lightly golden. Work in batches. Bon appétit!

# Barbecue Roasted Almonds

(Ready in about 20 minutes | Servings 6)

**Per serving:**

340 Calories; 30.1g Fat; 11.5g Carbs; 11.3g Protein; 2.3g Sugars

## Ingredients

1 ½ cups raw almonds

Sea salt and ground black pepper, to taste 1/4 teaspoon garlic powder

1/4 teaspoon mustard powder 1/2 teaspoon cumin powder 1/4 teaspoon smoked paprika 1 tablespoon olive oil

## Directions

Toss all Ingredients in a mixing bowl.

Line the Air Fryer basket with baking parchment. Spread out the coated almonds in a single layer in the basket.

Roast at 350 degrees F for 6 to 8 minutes, shaking the basket once or twice. Work in batches. Enjoy!

# Barbecue Tofu with Green Beans

(Ready in about 1 hour | Servings 3)

**Per serving:**

316 Calories; 19.8g Fat; 20.8g Carbs; 20.1g Protein; 8.1g Sugars

## Ingredients

12 ounces super firm tofu, pressed and cubed 1/4 cup ketchup

1 tablespoon white vinegar

1 tablespoon coconut sugar 1 tablespoon mustard

1/4 teaspoon ground black pepper

1/2 teaspoon sea salt

1/4 teaspoon smoked paprika

1/2 teaspoon freshly grated ginger 2 cloves garlic, minced

2 tablespoons olive oil 1 pound green beans

## Directions

Toss the tofu with the ketchup, white vinegar, coconut sugar, mustard, black pepper, sea salt, paprika, ginger, garlic, and olive oil. Let it marinate for 30 minutes.

Cook at 360 degrees F for 10 minutes; turn them over and cook for 12 minutes more. Reserve.

Place the green beans in the lightly greased Air Fryer basket. Roast at 400 degrees F for 5 minutes. Bon appétit!

# Butternut Squash Chili

(Ready in about 35 minutes | Servings 4)

**Per serving:**

295 Calories; 18.9g Fat; 29.3g Carbs; 7g Protein; 4.6g Sugars

## Ingredients

2 tablespoons canola oil 1 cup leeks, chopped

2 garlic cloves, crushed

2 ripe tomatoes, pureed

2 chipotle peppers in adobo, chopped 1 teaspoon ground cumin

1 teaspoon chili powder

Kosher salt and ground black pepper, to your liking 1 cup vegetable broth

1 pound butternut squash, peeled and diced into 1/2-inch chunks 16 ounces canned kidney beans, drained and rinsed

1 avocado, pitted, peeled and diced

## Directions

Start by preheating your Air Fryer to 365 degrees F.

Heat the oil in a baking pan until sizzling. Then, sauté the leeks and garlic in the baking pan. Cook for 4 to 6 minutes.

Now, add the tomatoes, chipotle peppers, cumin, chili powder, salt, pepper, and vegetable broth. Cook for 15 minutes, stirring every 5 minutes.

Stir in the the butternut squash and canned beans; let it cook for a further 8 minutes, stirring halfway through the cooking time.

Serve in individual bowls, garnished with the avocado. Enjoy!

# Cauliflower, Broccoli and Chickpea Salad

(Ready in about 20 minutes + chilling time | Servings 4)

**Per serving:**

263 Calories; 15.8g Fat; 24.8g Carbs; 9.4g Protein; 6.1g Sugars

# Ingredients

1/2 pound cauliflower florets 1/2 pound broccoli florets Sea salt, to taste

1/2 teaspoon red pepper flakes 2 tablespoons soy sauce

2 tablespoons cider vinegar

1 teaspoon Dijon mustard

2 tablespoons extra-virgin olive oil

1 cup canned or cooked chickpeas, drained 1 avocado, pitted, peeled and sliced

1 small sized onion, peeled and sliced 1 garlic clove, minced

2 cups arugula

2 tablespoons sesame seeds, lightly toasted

## Directions

Start by preheating your Air Fryer to 400 degrees F.

Brush the cauliflower and broccoli florets with cooking spray.

Cook for 12 minutes, shaking the cooking basket halfway through the cooking time. Season with salt and red pepper.

In a mixing dish, whisk the soy sauce, cider vinegar, Dijon mustard, and olive oil. Dress the salad. Add the chickpeas, avocado, onion, garlic, and arugula.

Top with sesame seeds. Bon appétit!

# Cinnamon Sugar Tortilla Chips

(Ready in about 20 minutes | Servings 4)

**Per serving:**

270 Calories; 14.1g Fat; 32.7g Carbs; 3.8g Protein; 7.7g Sugars

## Ingredients

4 (10-inch) flour tortillas

1/4 cup vegan margarine, melted 1 ½ tablespoons ground cinnamon 1/4 cup caster sugar

## Directions

Slice each tortilla into eight slices. Brush the tortilla pieces with the melted margarine.

In a mixing bowl, thoroughly combine the cinnamon and sugar. Toss the cinnamon mixture with the tortillas.

Transfer to the cooking basket and cook at 360 degrees F for 8 minutes or until lightly golden. Work in batches.

They will crisp up as they cool. Serve and enjoy!

# Classic Baked Banana

(Ready in about 20 minutes | Servings 2)

**Per serving:**

202 Calories; 5.9g Fat; 40.2g Carbs; 1.1g Protein; 29g Sugars

## Ingredients

2 just-ripe bananas

2 teaspoons lime juice 2 tablespoons honey

1/4 teaspoon grated nutmeg 1/2 teaspoon ground cinnamon A pinch of salt

## Directions

Toss the banana with all Ingredients until well coated. Transfer your bananas to the parchment-lined cooking basket.

Bake in the preheated Air Fryer at 370 degrees F for 12 minutes, turning them over halfway through the cooking time. Enjoy!

# Corn on the Cob with Spicy Avocado Spread

(Ready in about 15 minutes | Servings 4)

**Per serving:**

234 Calories; 9.2g Fat; 37.9g Carbs; 7.2g Protein; 1.9g Sugars

## Ingredients

4 corn cobs

1 avocado, pitted, peeled and mashed 1 clove garlic, pressed

1 tablespoon fresh lime juice 1 tablespoon soy sauce

4 teaspoons nutritional yeast

1/2 teaspoon cayenne pepper 1/2 teaspoon dried dill

Sea salt and ground black pepper, to taste

1 teaspoon hot sauce

2 heaping tablespoons fresh cilantro leaves, roughly chopped

## Directions

Spritz the corn with cooking spray. Cook at 390 degrees F for 6 minutes, turning them over halfway through the cooking time.

In the meantime, mix the avocado, lime juice, soy sauce, nutritional yeast, cayenne pepper, dill, salt, black pepper, and hot sauce.

Spread the avocado mixture all over the corn on the cob. Garnish with fresh cilantro leaves. Bon appétit!

# Delicious Asparagus and Mushroom Fritters

(Ready in about 15 minutes | Servings 4)

## Per serving:

231 Calories; 12.7g Fat; 24g Carbs; 10.2g Protein; 6.3g Sugars

# Ingredients

1 pound asparagus spears 1 tablespoon canola oil

1 teaspoon paprika

Sea salt and freshly ground black pepper, to taste 1 teaspoon garlic powder

3 tablespoons scallions, chopped

1 cup button mushrooms, chopped 1/2 cup fresh breadcrumbs

1 tablespoon flax seeds, soaked in 2 tablespoons of water (vegan "egg")

4 tablespoons sun-dried tomato hummus

## Directions

Place the asparagus spears in the lightly greased cooking basket. Toss the asparagus with the canola oil, paprika, salt, and black pepper.

Cook in the preheated Air Fryer at 400 degrees F for 5 minutes. Chop the asparagus spears and add the garlic powder, scallions, mushrooms, breadcrumbs, and vegan "egg".

Mix until everything is well incorporated and form the asparagus mixture into patties.

Cook in the preheated Air Fryer at 400 degrees F for 5 minutes, flipping halfway through the cooking time. Serve with sun-dried tomato hummus. Bon appétit!

# Easy Granola with Raisins and Nuts

(Ready in about 40 minutes | Servings 8)

**Per serving:**

222 Calories; 14g Fat; 29.9g Carbs; 5.3g Protein; 11.3g Sugars

## Ingredients

2 cups rolled oats

1/2 cup walnuts, chopped 1/3 cup almonds chopped 1/4 cup raisins

1/4 cup whole wheat pastry flour 1/2 teaspoon cinnamon

1/4 teaspoon nutmeg, preferably freshly grated 1/2 teaspoon salt

1/3 cup coconut oil, melted

1/3 cup agave nectar

1/2 teaspoon coconut extract 1/2 teaspoon vanilla extract

## Directions

Thoroughly combine all Ingredients. Then, spread the mixture onto the Air Fryer trays. Spritz with cooking spray.

Bake at 230 degrees F for 25 minutes; rotate the trays and bake 10 to 15 minutes more.

This granola can be stored in an airtight container for up to 2 weeks. Enjoy!

# Easy Vegan "Chicken"

(Ready in about 20 minutes | Servings 4)

**Per serving:**

348 Calories; 12.1g Fat; 41.5g Carbs; 21.7g Protein; 4.5g Sugars

## Ingredients

8 ounces soy chunks 1/2 cup cornmeal

1/4 cup all-purpose flour

1 teaspoon cayenne pepper 1/2 teaspoon mustard powder 1 teaspoon celery seeds

Sea salt and ground black pepper, to taste

## Directions

Boil the soya chunks in lots of water in a saucepan over medium-high heat. Remove from the heat and let them soak for 10 minutes.

Drain, rinse, and squeeze off the excess water.

Mix the remaining Ingredients in a bowl. Roll the soy chunks over the breading mixture, pressing to adhere.

Arrange the soy chunks in the lightly greased Air Fryer basket.

Cook in the preheated Air Fryer at 390 degrees for 10 minutes, turning them over halfway through the cooking time; work in batches. Bon appétit!

# Garlic-Roasted Brussels Sprouts with Mustard

(Ready in about 20 minutes | Servings 3)

**Per serving:**

151 Calories; 9.6g Fat; 14.5g Carbs; 5.4g Protein; 3.4g Sugars

## Ingredients

1 pound Brussels sprouts, halved 2 tablespoons olive oil

Sea salt and freshly ground black pepper, to taste

2 garlic cloves, minced

1 tablespoon Dijon mustard

## Directions

Toss the Brussels sprouts with the olive oil, salt, black pepper, and garlic.

Roast in the preheated Air Fryer at 380 degrees F for 15 minutes, shaking the basket occasionally.

Serve with Dijon mustard and enjoy!

# Gourmet Wasabi Popcorn

(Ready in about 30 minutes | Servings 2)

**Per serving:**

149 Calories; 11.7g Fat; 9.7g Carbs; 1.3g Protein; 0.6g Sugars

## Ingredients

1/2 teaspoon brown sugar 1 teaspoon salt

1/2 teaspoon wasabi powder, sifted

1 tablespoon avocado oil

3 tablespoons popcorn kernels

## Directions

Add the dried corn kernels to the Air Fryer basket; toss with the remaining Ingredients.

Cook at 395 degrees F for 15 minutes, shaking the basket every 5 minutes. Work in two batches.

Taste, adjust the seasonings and serve immediately. Bon appétit!

# Baked Oatmeal with Berries

(Ready in about 30 minutes | Servings 4)

## Per serving:

387 Calories; 24.1g Fat; 52.5g Carbs; 8.4g Protein; 25.9g Sugars

## Ingredients

1 cup fresh strawberries 1/2 cup dried cranberries 1 ½ cups rolled oats

1/2 teaspoon baking powder A pinch of sea salt

A pinch of grated nutmeg

1/2 teaspoon ground cinnamon 1/2 teaspoon vanilla extract

4 tablespoons agave syrup

1 ½ cups coconut milk

## Directions

Spritz a baking pan with cooking spray.

Place 1/2 cup of strawberries on the bottom of the pan; place the cranberries over that.

In a mixing bowl, thoroughly combine the rolled oats, baking powder, salt, nutmeg, cinnamon, vanilla, agave syrup, and milk.

Pour the oatmeal mixtures over the fruits; allow it to soak for 15 minutes. Top with the remaining fruits.

Bake at 330 degrees F for 12 minutes. Serve warm or at room temperature. Enjoy!

# Greek-Style Roasted Vegetables

(Ready in about 25 minutes | Servings 3)

**Per serving:**

299 Calories; 12.9g Fat; 30.4g Carbs; 5.8g Protein; 12.5g Sugars

## Ingredients

1/2 pound butternut squash, peeled and cut into 1-inch chunks 1/2 pound cauliflower, cut into 1-inch florets

1/2 pound zucchini, cut into 1-inch chunks

1 red onion, sliced

2 bell peppers, cut into 1-inch chunks 2 tablespoons extra-virgin olive oil

1 cup dry white wine

1 teaspoon dried rosemary

Sea salt and freshly cracked black pepper, to taste 1/2 teaspoon dried basil

1 (28-ounce) canned diced tomatoes with juice 1/2 cup Kalamata olives, pitted

## Directions

Toss the vegetables with the olive oil, wine, rosemary, salt, black pepper, and basil until well coated.

Pour 1/2 of the canned diced tomatoes into a lightly greased baking dish; spread to cover the bottom of the baking dish.

Add the vegetables and top with the remaining diced tomatoes. Scatter the Kalamata olives over the top.

Bake in the preheated Air Fryer at 390 degrees F for 20 minutes, rotating the dish halfway through the cooking time. Serve warm and enjoy!

# Green Beans with Oyster Mushrooms

(Ready in about 20 minutes | Servings 3)

**Per serving:**

109 Calories; 6.4g Fat; 11.6g Carbs; 3.9g Protein; 2.9g Sugars

## Ingredients

1 tablespoon extra-virgin olive oil 2 garlic cloves, minced

1/2 cup scallions, chopped

2 cups oyster mushrooms, sliced

12 ounces fresh green beans, trimmed 1 tablespoon soy sauce

Sea salt and ground black pepper, to taste

## Directions

Start by preheating your Air Fryer to 390 degrees F. Heat the oil and sauté the garlic and scallions until tender and fragrant, about 5 minutes.

Add the remaining Ingredients and stir to combine well.

Increase the temperature to 400 degrees F and cook for a further 5 minutes. Serve warm.

# Healthy Mac and Cheese

(Ready in about 30 minutes | Servings 4)

**Per serving:**

449 Calories; 18.3g Fat; 55.5g Carbs; 14.2g Protein; 9.7g Sugars

## Ingredients

12 ounces elbow pasta 2 garlic cloves, minced

1/3 cup vegan margarine

1/3 cup chickpea flour

3/4 cup unsweetened almond milk

2 heaping tablespoons nutritional yeast 1/2 teaspoon curry powder

1/2 teaspoon mustard powder 1/2 teaspoon celery seeds

Sea salt and white pepper, to taste 1 ½ cups pasta water

1/2 cup seasoned breadcrumbs

1 heaping tablespoon Italian parsley, roughly chopped

## Directions

Bring a pot of salted water to a boil over high heat; turn the heat down to medium and add the elbow pasta.

Let it cook approximately 8 minutes. Drain and transfer to the lightly greased baking pan.

In a mixing dish, thoroughly combine the garlic, margarine, chickpea flour, milk, nutritional yeast, and spices. Add the pasta water and mix to combine well.

Pour the milk mixture into the baking pan; gently stir to combine. Top with the seasoned breadcrumbs.

Bake in the preheated Air Fryer at 360 degrees F for 15 minutes. Serve garnished with fresh parsley leaves. Bon appétit!

# Herb Roasted Potatoes and Peppers

(Ready in about 30 minutes | Servings 4)

**Per serving:**

158 Calories; 6.8g Fat; 22.6g Carbs; 1.8g Protein; 2.2g Sugars

## Ingredients

1 pound russet potatoes, cut into 1-inch chunks

2 bell peppers, seeded and cut into 1-inch chunks 2 tablespoons olive oil

1 teaspoon dried rosemary 1 teaspoon dried basil

1 teaspoon dried oregano

1 teaspoon dried parsley flakes

Sea salt and ground black pepper, to taste 1/2 teaspoon smoked paprika

## Directions

Toss all Ingredients in the Air Fryer basket.

Roast at 400 degrees F for 15 minutes, tossing the basket occasionally. Work in batches.

Serve warm and enjoy!

# Hoisin-Glazed Bok Choy

(Ready in about 10 minutes | Servings 4)

**Per serving:**

235 Calories; 11.2g Fat; 6g Carbs; 25.7g Protein; 2.2g Sugars

## Ingredients

1 pound baby Bok choy, bottoms removed, leaves separated 2 garlic cloves, minced

1 teaspoon onion powder

1/2 teaspoon sage

2 tablespoons hoisin sauce 2 tablespoons sesame oil

1 tablespoon all-purpose flour

## Directions

Place the Bok choy, garlic, onion powder, and sage in the lightly greased Air Fryer basket.

Cook in the preheated Air Fryer at 350 degrees F for 3 minutes.

In a small mixing dish, whisk the hoisin sauce, sesame oil, and flour. Drizzle the sauce over the Bok choy. Cook for a further 3 minutes. Bon appétit!

# Hungarian Mushroom Pilaf

(Ready in about 50 minutes | Servings 4)

**Per serving:**

566 Calories; 19.1g Fat; 72.8g Carbs; 24.6g Protein; 7.2g Sugars

## Ingredients

1 ½ cups white rice

3 cups vegetable broth 2 tablespoons olive oil

1 pound fresh porcini mushrooms, sliced 2 tablespoons olive oil

2 garlic cloves

1 onion, chopped

1/4 cup dry vermouth 1 teaspoon dried thyme

1/2 teaspoon dried tarragon

1 teaspoon sweet Hungarian paprika

## Directions

Place the rice and broth in a large saucepan, add water; and bring to a boil. Cover, turn the heat down to low, and continue cooking for 16 to 18 minutes more. Set aside for 5 to 10 minutes.

Now, stir the hot cooked rice with the remaining Ingredients in a lightly greased baking dish.

Cook in the preheated Air Fryer at 370 degrees for 20 minutes, checking periodically to ensure even cooking.

Serve in individual bowls. Bon appétit!

# Indian Plantain Chips (Kerala Neenthram)

(Ready in about 30 minutes | Servings 2)

**Per serving:**

263 Calories; 9.4g Fat; 49.2g Carbs; 1.5g Protein; 21.3g Sugars

# Ingredients

1 pound plantain, thinly sliced 1 tablespoon turmeric

2 tablespoons coconut oil

## Directions

Fill a large enough cup with water and add the turmeric to the water.

Soak the plantain slices in the turmeric water for 15 minutes. Brush with coconut oil and transfer to the Air Fryer basket.

Cook in the preheated Air Fryer at 400 degrees F for 10 minutes, shaking the cooking basket halfway through the cooking time.

Serve at room temperature. Enjoy!

# Italian-Style Risi e Bisi

(Ready in about 20 minutes | Servings 4)

**Per serving:**

434 Calories; 8.3g Fat; 79.8g Carbs; 9.9g Protein; 5g Sugars

## Ingredients

2 cups brown rice 4 cups water

1/2 cup frozen green peas

3 tablespoons soy sauce 1 tablespoon olive oil

1 cup brown mushrooms, sliced

2 garlic cloves, minced

1 small-sized onion, chopped

1 tablespoon fresh parsley, chopped

## Directions

Heat the brown rice and water in a pot over high heat. Bring it to a boil; turn the stove down to simmer and cook for 35 minutes. Allow your rice to cool completely.

Transfer the cold cooked rice to the lightly greased Air Fryer pan. Add the remaining Ingredients and stir to combine.

Cook in the preheated Air Fryer at 360 degrees F for 18 to 22 minutes. Serve warm.

# Kid-Friendly Vegetable Fritters

(Ready in about 20 minutes | Servings 4)

## Per serving:

299 Calories; 11.3g Fat; 44.1g Carbs; 7.9g Protein; 4.6g Sugars

## Ingredients

1 pound broccoli florets

1 tablespoon ground flaxseeds 1 yellow onion, finely chopped

1 sweet pepper, seeded and chopped 1 carrot, grated

2 garlic cloves, pressed

1 teaspoon turmeric powder 1/2 teaspoon ground cumin 1/2 cup all-purpose flour 1/2 cup cornmeal

Salt and ground black pepper, to taste 2 tablespoons olive oil

## Directions

Blanch the broccoli in salted boiling water until al dente, about 3 to 4 minutes. Drain well and transfer to a mixing bowl; mash the broccoli florets with the remaining Ingredients.

Form the mixture into patties and place them in the lightly greased Air Fryer basket.

Cook at 400 degrees F for 6 minutes, turning them over halfway through the cooking time; work in batches.

Serve warm with your favorite Vegenaise. Enjoy!

# Marinated Tofu Bowl with Pearl Onions

(Ready in about 1 hour 20 minutes | Servings 4)

**Per serving:**

296 Calories; 16.7g Fat; 23.2g Carbs; 18.1g Protein; 14.1g Sugars

**Ingredients**

16 ounces firm tofu, pressed and cut into 1-inch pieces 2 tablespoons vegan Worcestershire sauce

1 tablespoon apple cider vinegar

1 tablespoon maple syrup 1/2 teaspoon shallot powder 1/2 teaspoon porcini powder 1/2 teaspoon garlic powder 2 tablespoons peanut oil

1 cup pearl onions, peeled

## Directions

Place the tofu, Worcestershire sauce, vinegar, maple syrup, shallot powder, porcini powder, and garlic powder in a ceramic dish. Let it marinate in your refrigerator for 1 hour.

Transfer the tofu to the lightly greased Air Fryer basket. Add the peanut oil and pearl onions; toss to combine.

Cook the tofu with the pearl onions in the preheated Air Fryer at 380 degrees F for 6 minutes; pause and brush with the reserved marinade; cook for a further 5 minutes.

Serve immediately. Bon appétit!

# Mashed Potatoes with Roasted Peppers

(Ready in about 1 hour | Servings 4)

## Per serving:

490 Calories; 17g Fat; 79.1g Carbs; 10.5g Protein; 9.8g Sugars

## Ingredients

4 potatoes

1 tablespoon vegan margarine 1 teaspoon garlic powder

1 pound bell peppers, seeded and quartered lengthwise 2 Fresno peppers, seeded and halved lengthwise

4 tablespoons olive oil

2 tablespoons cider vinegar 4 garlic cloves, pressed Kosher salt, to taste

1/2 teaspoon freshly ground black pepper 1/2 teaspoon dried dill

## Directions

Place the potatoes in the Air Fryer basket and cook at 400 degrees F for 40 minutes. Discard the skin and mash the potatoes with the vegan margarine and garlic powder.

Then, roast the peppers at 400 degrees F for 5 minutes. Give the peppers a half turn; place them back in the cooking basket and roast for another 5 minutes.

Turn them one more time and roast until the skin is charred and soft or 5 more minutes. Peel the peppers and let them cool to room temperature.

Toss your peppers with the remaining Ingredients and serve with the mashed potatoes. Bon appétit!

# Mediterranean-Style Potato Chips with Vegveeta Dip

(Ready in about 1 hour | Servings 4)

**Per serving:**

244 Calories; 18g Fat; 19.4g Carbs; 4g Protein; 1.7g Sugars

## Ingredients

1 large potato, cut into 1/8 inch thick slices 1 tablespoon olive oil

Sea salt, to taste

1/2 teaspoon red pepper flakes, crushed 1 teaspoon fresh rosemary

1/2 teaspoon fresh sage

1/2 teaspoon fresh basil Dipping Sauce:

1/3 cup raw cashews

1 tablespoon tahini

1 ½ tablespoons olive oil 1/4 cup raw almonds

1/4 teaspoon prepared yellow mustard

## Directions

Soak the potatoes in a large bowl of cold water for 20 to 30 minutes. Drain the potatoes and pat them dry with a kitchen towel. Toss with olive oil and seasonings.

Place in the lightly greased cooking basket and cook at 380 degrees F for 30 minutes. Work in batches.

Meanwhile, puree the sauce Ingredients in your food processor until smooth. Serve the potato chips with the Vegveeta sauce for dipping. Bon appétit!

# Onion Rings with Spicy Ketchup

(Ready in about 30 minutes | Servings 2)

## Per serving:

361 Calories; 4.5g Fat; 67.5g Carbs; 12.1g Protein; 10.5g Sugars

## Ingredients

1 onion, sliced into rings 1/3 cup all-purpose flour 1/2 cup oat milk

1 teaspoon curry powder

1 teaspoon cayenne pepper

Salt and ground black pepper, to your liking 1/2 cup cornmeal

4 tablespoons vegan parmesan 1/4 cup spicy ketchup

## Directions

Place the onion rings in the bowl with cold water; let them soak approximately 20 minutes; drain the onion rings and pat dry using a kitchen towel.

In a shallow bowl, mix the flour, milk, curry powder, cayenne pepper, salt, and black pepper. Mix to combine well.

Mix the cornmeal and vegan parmesan in another shallow bowl. Dip the onion rings in the flour/milk mixture; then, dredge in the cornmeal mixture.

Spritz the Air Fryer basket with cooking spray; arrange the breaded onion rings in the Air Fryer basket.

Cook in the preheated Air Fryer at 400 degrees F for 4 to 5 minutes, turning them over halfway through the cooking time. Serve with spicy ketchup. Bon appétit!

# Paprika Brussels Sprout Chips

(Ready in about 20 minutes | Servings 2)

**Per serving:**

64 Calories; 2.6g Fat; 9.1g Carbs; 3.3g Protein; 2.2g Sugars

## Ingredients

10 Brussels sprouts 1 teaspoon canola oil

1 teaspoon coarse sea salt

1 teaspoon paprika

## Directions

Toss all Ingredients in the lightly greased Air Fryer basket.

Bake at 380 degrees F for 15 minutes, shaking the basket halfway through the cooking time to ensure even cooking.

Serve and enjoy!

# Rosemary Au Gratin Potatoes

(Ready in about 45 minutes | Servings 4)

## Per serving:

386 Calories; 15.7g Fat; 50.5g Carbs; 14.3g Protein; 6.1g Sugars

## Ingredients

2 pounds potatoes

1/4 cup sunflower kernels, soaked overnight 1/2 cup almonds, soaked overnight

1 cup unsweetened almond milk 2 tablespoons nutritional yeast 1 teaspoon shallot powder

2 fresh garlic cloves, minced 1/2 cup water

Kosher salt and ground black pepper, to taste

1 teaspoon cayenne pepper 1 tablespoon fresh rosemary

## Directions

Bring a large pan of water to a boil. Cook the whole potatoes for about 20 minutes. Drain the potatoes and let sit until cool enough to handle.

Peel your potatoes and slice into 1/8-inch rounds.

Add the sunflower kernels, almonds, almond milk, nutritional yeast, shallot powder, and garlic to your food processor; blend until uniform, smooth, and creamy. Add the water and blend for 30 seconds more.

Place 1/2 of the potatoes overlapping in a single layer in the lightly greased casserole dish. Spoon 1/2 of the sauce on top of the potatoes. Repeat the layers, ending with the sauce.

Top with salt, black pepper, cayenne pepper, and fresh rosemary. Bake in the preheated Air Fryer at 325 degrees F for 20 minutes. Serve warm.

# Spicy Roasted Cashew Nuts

(Ready in about 20 minutes | Servings 4)

## Per serving:

400 Calories; 35.1g Fat; 19.3g Carbs; 7.7g Protein; 5.8g Sugars

## Ingredients

1 cup whole cashews 1 teaspoon olive oil

Salt and ground black pepper, to taste

1/2 teaspoon smoked paprika 1/2 teaspoon ancho chili powder

## Directions

Toss all Ingredients in the mixing bowl.

Line the Air Fryer basket with baking parchment. Spread out the spiced cashews in a single layer in the basket.

Roast at 350 degrees F for 6 to 8 minutes, shaking the basket once or twice. Work in batches. Enjoy!

# Sunday Potato Fritters

(Ready in about 30 minutes | Servings 3)

**Per serving:**

367 Calories; 8.9g Fat; 60.6g Carbs; 12.8g Protein; 7.5g Sugars

**Ingredients**

1 tablespoon olive oil

1/2 pound potatoes, peeled and cut into chunks 1/2 cup cashew cream

1/2 cup chickpea flour

1/2 teaspoon baking powder 1/2 onion, chopped

1 garlic clove, minced

Sea salt and ground black pepper, to your liking 1 cup tortilla chips, crushed

## Directions

Start by preheating your Air Fryer to 400 degrees F.

Drizzle the olive oil all over the potatoes. Place the potatoes in the Air Fryer basket and cook approximately 15 minutes, shaking the basket periodically.

Lightly crush the potatoes to split; mash the potatoes and combine with the other Ingredients. Form the potato mixture into patties.

Bake in the preheated Air Fryer at 380 degrees F for 14 minutes, flipping them halfway through the cooking time to ensure even cooking. Bon appétit!

# The Best Falafel Ever

(Ready in about 20 minutes | Servings 2)

## Per serving:

411 Calories; 6.1g Fat; 70.2g Carbs; 21.4g Protein; 12.2g Sugars

## Ingredients

1 cup dried chickpeas, soaked overnight 1 small-sized onion, chopped

2 cloves garlic, minced

2 tablespoons fresh cilantro leaves, chopped 1 tablespoon flour

1/2 teaspoon baking powder

1 teaspoon cumin powder

A pinch of ground cardamom

Sea salt and ground black pepper, to taste

## Directions

Pulse all the Ingredients in your food processor until the chickpeas are ground.

Form the falafel mixture into balls and place them in the lightly greased Air Fryer basket.

Cook at 380 degrees F for about 15 minutes, shaking the basket occasionally to ensure even cooking.

Serve in pita bread with toppings of your choice. Enjoy!

# Tofu and Brown Rice Bake

(Ready in about 55 minutes + marinating time| Servings 4)

## Per serving:

402 Calories; 14.7g Fat; 54.7g Carbs; 15.3g Protein; 8.3g Sugars

## Ingredients

1 cup brown rice

16 ounces extra firm tofu, pressed, drained, and cut into bite-sized cubes
Marinade:

2 tablespoons sesame oil 1/2 cup tamari sauce

2 tablespoons maple syrup

1 tablespoon white vinegar 1 teaspoon hot sauce

4 tablespoons cornstarch

Salt and black pepper, to taste

## Directions

Heat the brown rice and 2 ½ cups of water in a saucepan over high heat. Bring it to a boil; turn the stove down to simmer and cook for 35 minutes.

Place the tofu in a ceramic dish; add the remaining Ingredients for the marinade and whisk to combine well. Allow it to marinate for 1 hour in your refrigerator.

Grease a baking pan with nonstick cooking spray. Add the hot rice and place the tofu on the top. Stir in the reserved marinade.

Cook at 370 degrees F for 15 minutes, checking occasionally to ensure even cooking. Enjoy!

# Tofu in Sweet & Sour Sauce

(Ready in about 25 minutes | Servings 3)

## Per serving:

171 Calories; 7.1g Fat; 13.2g Carbs; 14.4g Protein; 6.2g Sugars

## Ingredients

2 tablespoons Shoyu sauce

16 ounces extra-firm tofu, drained, pressed and cubed 1/2 cup water

1/4 cup pineapple juice 2 garlic cloves, minced

1/2 teaspoon fresh ginger, grated

1 teaspoon cayenne pepper

1/4 teaspoon ground black pepper 1/2 teaspoon salt

1 teaspoon honey

1 tablespoon arrowroot powder

## Directions

Drizzle the Shoyu sauce all over the tofu cubes. Cook in the preheated Air Fryer at 380 degrees F for 6 minutes; shake the basket and cook for a further 5 minutes.

Meanwhile, cook the remaining Ingredients in a heavy skillet over medium heat for 10 minutes, until the sauce has slightly thickened.

Stir the fried tofu into the sauce and continue cooking for 4 minutes more or until the tofu is thoroughly heated.

Serve warm and enjoy!

# Thai Sweet Potato Balls

(Ready in about 50 minutes | Servings 4)

## Per serving:

286 Calories; 6.1g Fat; 56.8g Carbs; 3.1g Protein; 33.7g Sugars

## Ingredients

1 pound sweet potatoes 1 cup brown sugar

1 tablespoon orange juice

2 teaspoons orange zest

1/2 teaspoon ground cinnamon 1/4 teaspoon ground cloves 1/2 cup almond meal

1 teaspoon baking powder 1 cup coconut flakes

## Directions

Bake the sweet potatoes at 380 degrees F for 30 to 35 minutes until tender; peel and mash them.

Add the brown sugar, orange juice, orange zest, ground cinnamon, cloves, almond meal, and baking powder; mix to combine well.

Roll the balls in the coconut flakes.

Bake in the preheated Air Fryer at 360 degrees F for 15 minutes or until thoroughly cooked and crispy.

Repeat the process until you run out of Ingredients. Bon appétit!

# Ultimate Vegan Calzone

(Ready in about 25 minutes | Servings 1)

## Per serving:

535 Calories; 14g Fat; 88.2g Carbs; 16g Protein; 19g Sugars

## Ingredients

1 teaspoon olive oil

1/2 small onion, chopped

2 sweet peppers, seeded and sliced Sea salt, to taste

1/4 teaspoon ground black pepper 1/4 teaspoon dried oregano

4 ounces prepared Italian pizza dough 1/4 cup marinara sauce

2 ounces plant-based cheese Mozzarella-style, shredded

## Directions

Heat the olive oil in a nonstick skillet. Once hot, cook the onion and peppers until tender and fragrant, about 5 minutes. Add salt, black pepper, and oregano.

Sprinkle some flour on a kitchen counter and roll out the pizza dough.

Spoon the marinara sauce over half of the dough; add the sautéed mixture and sprinkle with the vegan cheese. Now, gently fold over the dough to create a pocket; make sure to seal the edges.

Use a fork to poke the dough in a few spots. Add a few drizzles of olive oil and place in the lightly greased cooking basket.

Bake in the preheated Air Fryer at 330 degrees F for 12 minutes, turning the calzones over halfway through the cooking time. Bon appétit!

# Vegetable Kabobs with Simple Peanut Sauce

(Ready in about 30 minutes | Servings 4)

## Per serving:

323 Calories; 8.8g Fat; 56g Carbs; 7.6g Protein; 11.5g Sugars

## Ingredients

8 whole baby potatoes, diced into 1-inch pieces 2 bell peppers, diced into 1-inch pieces

8 pearl onions, halved

8 small button mushrooms, cleaned 2 tablespoons extra-virgin olive oil

Sea salt and ground black pepper, to taste

1 teaspoon red pepper flakes, crushed 1 teaspoon dried rosemary, crushed 1/3 teaspoon granulated garlic

Peanut Sauce:

2 tablespoons peanut butter

1 tablespoon balsamic vinegar 1 tablespoon soy sauce

1/2 teaspoon garlic salt

## Directions

Soak the wooden skewers in water for 15 minutes.

Thread the vegetables on skewers; drizzle the olive oil all over the vegetable skewers; sprinkle with spices.

Cook in the preheated Air Fryer at 400 degrees F for 13 minutes.

Meanwhile, in a small dish, whisk the peanut butter with the balsamic vinegar, soy sauce, and garlic salt. Serve your kabobs with the peanut sauce on the side. Enjoy!

# Warm Farro Salad with Roasted Tomatoes

(Ready in about 40 minutes | Servings 2)

## Per serving:

452 Calories; 14.5g Fat; 72.9g Carbs; 7.7g Protein; 9.5g Sugars

**Ingredients** 3/4 cup farro 3 cups water

1 tablespoon sea salt

1 pound cherry tomatoes 2 spring onions, chopped 2 carrots, grated

2 heaping tablespoons fresh parsley leaves 2 tablespoons champagne vinegar

2 tablespoons white wine

2 tablespoons extra-virgin olive oil 1 teaspoon red pepper flakes

## Directions

Place the farro, water, and salt in a saucepan and bring it to a rapid boil. Turn the heat down to medium-low, and simmer, covered, for 30 minutes or until the farro has softened.

Drain well and transfer to an air fryer-safe pan.

Meanwhile, place the cherry tomatoes in the lightly greased Air Fryer basket. Roast at 400 degrees F for 4 minutes.

Add the roasted tomatoes to the pan with the cooked farro, Toss the salad Ingredients with the spring onions, carrots, parsley, vinegar, white wine, and olive oil.

Bake at 360 degrees F an additional 5 minutes. Serve garnished with red pepper flakes and enjoy!

# Winter Squash and Tomato Bake

(Ready in about 30 minutes | Servings 4)

## Per serving:

330 Calories; 25.3g Fat; 23.2g Carbs; 8.5g Protein; 3.2g Sugars

## Ingredients

Cashew Cream:

1/2 cup sunflower seeds, soaked overnight, rinsed and drained 1/4 cup lime juice

Sea salt, to taste

2 teaspoons nutritional yeast 1 tablespoon tahini

1/2 cup water Squash:

1 pound winter squash, peeled and sliced

2 tablespoons olive oil

Sea salt and ground black pepper, to taste Sauce:

2 tablespoons olive oil 2 ripe tomatoes, crushed

6 ounces spinach, torn into small pieces

2 garlic cloves, minced 1 cup vegetable broth

1/2 teaspoon dried rosemary 1/2 teaspoon dried basil

## Directions

Mix the Ingredients for the cashew cream in your food processor until creamy and uniform. Reserve.

Place the squash slices in the lightly greased casserole dish. Add the olive oil, salt, and black pepper.

Mix all the Ingredients for the sauce. Pour the sauce over the vegetables. Bake in the preheated Air Fryer at 390 degrees F for 15 minutes.

Top with the cashew cream and bake an additional 5 minutes or until everything is thoroughly heated.

Transfer to a wire rack to cool slightly before sling and serving.

# Alphabetical Index

## W

CPSIA information can be obtained
at www.ICGtesting.com
Printed in the USA
LVHW020406120521
687183LV00008B/833